the little Sleeping Beauty

LUKE 8:40-42, 49-56 FOR CHILDREN

Written by Brenda Grace Prior

Illustrated by Alice Hausner

ARCH Books

CONCORDIA PUBLISHING HOUSE LTD., LONDON, E. C. 1
MANUFACTURED IN THE UNITED STATES OF AMERICA

ISBN-0-570-06041-9

One day at sunrise,
when the moon had faded
and the brown hills were
turned to gold,

a little boat came bobbing
across the shining Sea of Galilee.

And on the shore
a crowd of people,
like a rushing tide,
ran down to welcome Jesus.

Many of them were poor
and many old and sick;
barefoot beggars dressed in rags,
and noisy children
pushing and shoving the fine ladies,
stepping on the toes of wealthy merchants,
craning their necks
to see the quiet Man
whose face was turned to greet them
and whose eyes were full of pity.

And Jesus, standing tall
among His robed disciples,
stretched out His gentle hands to heal
the blind, the sick, the lame.

Then
suddenly
pushing his way
through the crowd,
came a well-dressed man,
Jairus, president of a Jewish church,
a great man, known to all.
The people, bowing, stood aside to let him pass

Then Jairus, in his splendid robes,
knelt down in the dust
at the feet of Jesus.

"Master," he said, "my little girl,
my only child, is ill,
and if You do not come at once
and heal her,
she will surely die."

As he spoke, his face
was wrinkled up with grief.

So Jesus went with Jairus,
and the people followed
to see what He would do.

But as they walked along
the dry, hard path
beside the deep-blue sea,

a man came to tell Jairus
that his little girl was dead
and there was no need
to trouble Jesus anymore.

But Jesus said,
"Have no fear; only have faith.
She will be well."
And taking His friends
Peter, James, and John,
He followed Jairus to the big, white house
shaded by palm trees from the noonday sun.

Everyone was crying and wailing.
The mother was sobbing.

Her little girl would be there no more to play in the bright garden, singing like a bird beside the silver fountain.

The tall, white-robed Stranger,
without so much as looking at the child,
said calmly, "Do not weep.
The little girl's not dead; she is asleep."

"Asleep!" the people laughed.
As if the doctors did not know better than He!

But
Jesus
sent
them
all
outside.

Then, with the parents at His side
and His three friends following,
He went into the low, cool room
where the little maiden lay.

"My child," He said
and gently took her hand,
"I say to you,
Arise!"

And the little girl sat up,
then danced around the room
and kissed her parents,
who were crying now for joy.

Then Jesus said, "Give her some food."

He asked Jairus and his wife
to tell no one
what He had done.

But others knew and told.
And many people heard
how Jesus brought the little girl to life
to play and sing again
around the silver fountain
in her happy parents' garden.

DEAR PARENTS:

Death is a sorrowful experience, but the death of a child causes the deepest sense of grief and loss. It seems cruel and senseless to see a beautiful child die of a painful disease or in an accident. Our civilization has tried to cover the ugliness of death with flowers, cosmetics, and caskets, but the reality of death cannot be hidden, especially from a child.

Because Adam sinned, death came into the world and has spread to all men, as Paul says in Romans 5:12. The Scriptures do not try to hide death or make it pretty; they take death seriously. Death is real.

But life is real too, and the victory over death is real. God became man and lived among us. Jesus Christ, the Son of God, died in our place. By His resurrection He overcame death for us.

Even before His own resurrection Jesus revealed His power over death by restoring life to the 12-year-old daughter of Jairus. The father of the "Little Sleeping Beauty" believed that Jesus was the strong Son of God who could help.

You can help your child understand death by answering his questions honestly. More important, you can give your child hope as you share your faith in the living Christ, who overcame death and will raise you from death to everlasting life.

THE EDITOR